WEST CORK
the guide

PHOTOGRAPHS AND TEXT BY
JOHN J. EARLEY

First published in 1998 by Earlybird Productions

ISBN 0 9532607 0 4

Produced by Earlybird Productions, Skibbereen, Co. Cork
Dec O'Donovan Design • City Print, Cork.

CONTENTS

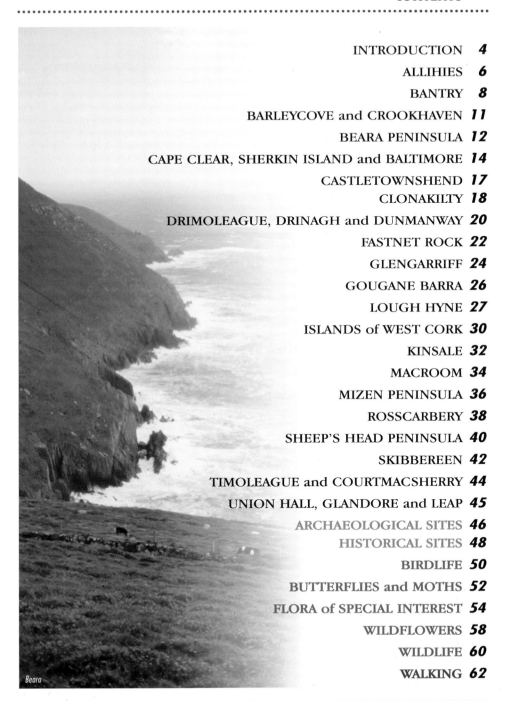

Beara

INTRODUCTION *to* WEST CORK

West Cork is situated on the south coast of Ireland between Kinsale and Ardgroom and is the most south-westerly part of Ireland. Sparsely populated, it is wild, unspoilt and a place of great scenic beauty. From east to west the region is 130 km wide and 100 km from north to south.

West Cork is far removed from the hustle and bustle of the busy world. With its picturesque scenery, fresh Atlantic air and a gentle pace of life, West Cork is the ideal place to relax. There are few places in Ireland where you will encounter such a genteel and friendly people as the inhabitants of West Cork.

West Cork has a wealth of appealing places to visit and things to see including offshore islands, towns, villages, historic castles, archaeological sites and attractive flora and fauna.

Discover West Cork, where centuries of history come together in one small place.

This guide is designed to acquaint the visitor with some of the charming features of this wonderful part of Ireland.

COUNTY CORK (some facts and figures)

Cork (Irish: *Corcaigh*) is a county in the province of Munster in southern Ireland on the Atlantic coast. It is the largest Irish county, covering just over 7,500 sq. km. (1.9 million acres), almost one-tenth of Ireland. County Cork has a population of over 400,000, with more than one-third living in the city of Cork and 50,000 approx. in West Cork.

Cork is bounded by the Atlantic Ocean (south), Counties Waterford and Tipperary (east), Co. Limerick (north), and Co. Kerry (west).

Local administration is by County Council and County Manager with three management divisions of North, South and West Cork. Cork City is administered by Corporation and City Manager.

CLIMATE

The West Cork climate is very mild due to the influence of the Atlantic Ocean and the warm waters of the Gulf Stream. In summer, sea breezes keep land temperatures moderately cool, while in winter severe frost or heavy snow is extremely rare. Mean air temperatures range from 6°C in winter to 15°C in summer. Extremes of heat or cold are virtually unknown. The prevailing south-westerly winds often bring soft oceanic drizzle. Total rainfall amounts to about 1250mm (50 inches) per annum.

COASTLINE

The pristine waters of the Atlantic Ocean bathe the coast of West Cork. The heavily indented coastline from Kinsale to Ardgroom is almost 750 km long and has many scenic bays and inlets. The beautiful bays of Bantry, Dunmanus and Roaringwater surround the picturesque peninsulas of Beara, Mizen and Sheep's Head. The coastline features several golden beaches with excellent water quality: many have been awarded the International Blue Flag. Water temperature in summer can reach 19°C and drop to 10°C in winter. Care should be taken as some beaches may be unsafe for swimming.

There are several offshore inhabited islands, accessible and worth exploring.

West Cork has many small harbours and is close to important international shipping lanes. Old watch-towers, signal-stations and lighthouses dot the coastline.

Near Toe Head

LANDSCAPE

The geological formation of West Cork is largely of Old Red Sandstone, with a rugged landscape shaped in the Ice Age. This landscape is very imposing with rocky mountains, green countryside, rivers, streams, mountain lakes and miles of striking coastline.

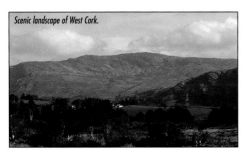
Scenic landscape of West Cork.

HISTORIC WEST CORK

In West Cork the O'Driscoll clan were the ancient rulers, descendants of the Milesians. The Milesians are said to have come from northern Spain about 1700 BC. Other prominent clans in West Cork include McCarthys, O'Donovans, O'Learys, O'Mahonys and O'Sullivans. Several old castles (in ruins) remind us of the time these great Irish chieftains ruled in the region. Much of the area known today as West Cork was originally called the Barony of Carbery. The name Carbery is said to derive from Corca Luighe, meaning the territory of the tribe of Luighe.

Other Baronies in West Cork include Bantry, Beara, Courceys, Ibane and Barryroe, and Kinsale.

During the Great Potato Famine of the 1840s many West Cork people died of hunger and disease, many more emigrated to the four corners of the globe.

FAMOUS NATIVES OF WEST CORK

O'Sullivan Beare was the local chieftain of the Beara Peninsula. After the Battle of Kinsale (1601) and the defeat of the Irish, O'Sullivan Beare, with the remnants of his clan, made his famous Long March from Glengarriff to Leitrim, over 300km, in 15 days.

The father of Henry Ford, founder of the automobile company, lived near Ballinascarty, Clonakilty before emigrating to America in the 1840s.

The Irish patriot Jeremiah O'Donovan-Rossa (1831-1915) was born near Rosscarbery.

Bantry born Tim Healy (1855-1931) became the first Governor-General of the Irish Free State in 1922.

Sam Maguire (1879-1927), who lent his name to the Gaelic Football Trophy, was born near Dunmanway.

Michael Collins (1890-1922), one of the heroes of the struggle for Irish Independence, was born at Woodfield near Clonakilty.

Edith Somerville, with Violet Ross, penned the humorous books on the exploits of the Irish R.M. (Resident Magistrate) Edith was born and resided until her death in Castletownshend.

Fuchsia

FUCHSIA

The Fuchsia (Fuchsia magellanica) is a bushy shrub, native to South America and introduced to Ireland. In the early 19th century it was planted widely in western Ireland for hedging, but has run wild in places. In its native South America hummingbirds feed on the rich store of nectar. The scarlet-and-purple blossoms of the Fuchsia decorate almost every hedgerow in West Cork from May to early November. Locally it is called 'Deora Dé' (Gaelic) or God's Teardrop.

High cliffs near Mizen Head

ALLIHIES

Allihies is situated on the west coast of the Beara Peninsula. It is a place of mountain, valley, sea and great scenic beauty. The mountains of Sliabh Miskish surround it on three sides and the Atlantic Ocean on the other. The coastline is indented with inlets, including Ballydonegan Bay and its sandy beach. Heading to Allihies from Castletownbere via Barnes Gap, the visitor can enjoy magnificent views of Ballydonegan Bay, the Kerry Mountains, Scarriff Island, Skellig Rocks and Allihies village nestling beneath the towering mountains: this is one of the most awe-inspiring vistas in the whole of Ireland. During the 20th century the population of Allihies has declined steadily due to emigration. Tourism, fishing and farming, particulary sheep, are the main enterprises in the area.

BALLYDONEGAN BEACH

The splendid beach at Ballydonegan contains coarse sand which is the residue of the grinding from copper mining in the area. It is an enjoyable place to relax but there can be an undercurrent in rough seas.

MINING for COPPER

In the 19th century Allihies was famous for copper mining. In 1810 copper was first discovered here by Colonel Hall. He devoted his time to searching for copper after his regiment was disbanded in 1802.
Local landlord John Puxley opened the first Allihies mines in 1812.

Ruined Coppermines near Allihies

At its peak in the mid 19th century, mining was extensive in the Allihies area, with up to 1000 people employed and almost 10,000 tons of copper mined per annum. Total output of 300,000 tons was recorded and the deepest shaft was 450 metres.
The mines closed in 1931, but in 1956 reopened temporarily; however, no ore was extracted. There is still some copper ore in the area but it is not economical to mine.
A few ruins and debris are all that remain today of the large industrial complex that grew up around Allihies in the 19th century.
The tall chimney that looks down on Allihies from the foothills of the mountain is the ruins of an engine house.
Today many of the old mining shafts are dangerous and should not be entered under any circumstances.

PREHISTORIC MINING

During the Bronze Age copper was mined at several locations in West Cork, including the Beara Peninsula. However, there is no evidence of mining in the Allihies area at this time.

Ballydonegan Beach

Allihies village

PLACES OF INTEREST

- Allihies and ruined Copper Mines
- Ballydonegan Beach
- Cable Car at Dursey Sound
- Dursey Island

BANTRY

The town of Bantry is located at the northern end of the bay to which it gives its name. Anciently called Kilgoban after its patron, St. Goban, the present name Bantry is said to derive from Beant-Mac-Farriola, a descendant of the O'Donovans and O'Mahonys, chieftains of the area. Today Bantry is a market town, port and tourist centre.

Bantry House

BANTRY HOUSE

Bantry House is situated on the verge of Bantry town and overlooks Bantry Bay. The original house was built in 1750 and was once the seat of the Earls of Bantry and is well worth a visit.

BANTRY BAY

Bantry Bay is a long inlet of the Atlantic Ocean and an area of outstanding natural beauty. The bay is 48 km long, 16 km at its broadest point and is one of the largest and deepest natural bays not only in Ireland but also in Europe.

Bantry Bay is surrounded by mountains and separates the Beara Peninsula to the north from the Sheep's Head Peninsula to the south. The bay gives good shelter to yachts and ships in adverse weather.

Bantry Bay featured prominently twice in the naval history of Ireland; in 1689 when a French fleet entered the bay to aid James II, and again in 1796 to assist the rebellion by The United Irishmen.

FRENCH ARMADA 1796

In the late 1700s the Irish patriot Theobold Wolfe Tone, of The United Irishmen, enlisted French assistance to overthrow British rule in Ireland. In December 1796 a French Armada with 15,000 troops left Brest in France for Bantry Bay. However, severe winter weather conditions scattered the fleet and only 19 ships with 6,500 troops arrived in the bay off Bere Island. Fierce easterly gales prevented a landing and blew the ships out to sea. By New Year's Day 1797, 12 ships with 4,500 troops were anchored off Whiddy Island. After many attempts and failing to land in Ireland, the fleet returned to France. One old frigate, *La Surveillante*, was left behind because of storm damage and was scuttled off Whiddy Island on January 2nd 1797.

The story of this ship and the unsuccessful French invasion is related in an exhibition at Bantry House.

PLACES OF INTEREST

- Armada Exhibition
- Bantry Bay
- Bantry House
- Whiddy Island

Fishing boats at Bantry

Bantry Bay and Bantry Town from Vaughan's Pass

FISHING

The main commercial fishing fleet in Bantry Bay is based at the port of Castletownbere, with a smaller fleet at Bantry. Castletownbere is one of the chief commercial fishing centres in Ireland.

Fish species regularly landed include cod, haddock, herring, mackerel, plaice, whiting and shellfish such as lobster, prawn, shrimp and scallop.

Mountains of Beara Peninsula

BANTRY BAY MUSSEL FARMING

In recent years Bantry Bay has become the most important area in Ireland for the production of mussels, which are grown on rope rafts in sheltered sections of the bay. Processing for sale takes place in local factories.

ISLANDS of BANTRY BAY

Within the vast open Bantry Bay there are a number of islands. The largest, **Bere Island**, is inhabited and has a long and interesting history. For many years it was an important British military and naval base. It is used today by the Irish army for training.

Garinish Island lies within Glengarriff Bay. It is famous for its landscaped gardens, particularly the Italian one, and is well worth a visit by boat from Glengarriff.

A low rock, **Roancarrig**, is the site of the only lighthouse in Bantry Bay.

Whiddy Island is the location of a large oil terminal and is home to several families who farm the fertile land.

Roancarrig Lighthouse

Whiddy Terminal

SIGHTSEEING of BANTRY BAY

Because of its vast size, it is difficult to view the whole of Bantry Bay at once, except perhaps from the air. Bantry Bay is surrounded by scenic mountains and magnificent views of the bay can be had from a number of good vantage points:

● VAUGHAN'S PASS

Vaughan's Pass (named after a County Councillor from the 1950s) is east of Bantry town off the Cork/ Drimoleague road (R586) and provides magnificent views of inner Bantry Bay and the islands.

● GLENGARRIFF ROAD LAYBY

On the road between Bantry town and Glengarriff (N71) there are a number of viewing points overlooking Bantry Bay where the visitor can enjoy wonderful views of the area. Viewing points between Bantry and Adrigole offer views of the Whiddy Island oil terminal and jetty. A point on the road west of Castletownbere also presents excellent views of the outer area of Bantry Bay and Castletownbere.

● SHEEP'S HEAD PENINSULA

The visitor travelling the narrow road on the north side of the Sheep's Head Peninsula will also encounter spectacular land and seascapes. From the tip of the peninsula at Sheep's Head, there are some impressive vistas of outer Bantry Bay and the Atlantic Ocean.

Sailing off Sheep's Head Peninsula

St. Brendan the Navigator at Bantry

WHIDDY ISLAND OIL TERMINAL

The oil terminal on Whiddy Island was constructed in 1969 by Gulf Oil. It was established at a time when the Suez canal was closed to shipping. Large crude-oil tankers, known as supertankers, sailed from the Middle East via the Cape of Good Hope to the Whiddy terminal to discharge their cargo. With large size and deep draft, many of these tankers could not enter most world ports, however Bantry Bay could accommodate them.

The first oil tanker to discharge at the terminal was the supertanker *Universe Ireland*. In 1979, the *Betelgeuse* was the last to discharge its cargo.

BETELGEUSE OIL TANKER

The French oil tanker *Betelgeuse* exploded on January 8th 1979 while unloading a cargo of crude oil at the terminal, with the unfortunate loss of fifty French and Irish lives. An inscribed memorial high-cross stands in the cemetery near Bantry town.

A single-point mooring buoy for loading and offloading has been installed since.

BARLEYCOVE
and
CROOKHAVEN

Barleycove is a series of delightful beaches at the far end of the Mizen Peninsula between the village of Crookhaven and Mizen Head.
The larger Barleycove Beach is surrounded on two sides by the high ground of Brow and Mizen Head and is one of the loveliest beaches in West Cork.
Impressive sand dunes and Lissagriffin Lake are found behind Barleycove Beach.

MIZEN FOG SIGNAL STATION

Mizen Head is close to Crookhaven. The Fog Signal Station is open to the public and well worth a visit.

LISSAGRIFFIN

The large shallow lake behind Barleycove Beach is of interest to birdwatchers. Many species of wading birds, ducks and swans frequent the lake in winter. However, it is most noted for rare bird species. In spring and autumn, Lissagriffin is an important stop-over and feeding area for migrating wading birds and terns. Many rare species have been spotted here over the years, including American species such as Pectoral Sandpiper.

BROW HEAD

Brow Head presents spectacular views of the Atlantic Ocean, Crookhaven, Fastnet Rock and Roaringwater Bay. The remains of the wireless station set up by Guglielmo Marconi can be seen at the summit.

CROOKHAVEN

Crookhaven is the southernmost village in Ireland. For centuries it had been a harbour and sea-port of fluctuating prosperity until steam replaced sail. Today it is a port of call for yachts from many countries. At the beginning of the 1900s, Guglielmo Marconi spent some time in the village while constructing a wireless station at Brow Head.

Crookhaven

PLACES OF INTEREST

- Barleycove Beach
- Brow Head
- Crookhaven Village
- Lissagriffin (Birdwatching)
- Mizen Head Fog Signal Station

Barleycove Beach

BEARA PENINSULA

Beara Peninsula is the most westerly part of County Cork. Bordered by the waters of Bantry Bay, Kenmare Bay and the Atlantic Ocean, it is the largest peninsula in County Cork.
Beara is dominated by the Caha Mountains, which run down the middle of the peninsula from end to end. With its rocky mountains, glacial lakes and rugged coastline, Beara is an area of great scenic beauty.
The principal villages and towns in Beara are: Allihies, Ardgroom, Castletownbere, Eyeries and Glengarriff.

ARCHAEOLOGICAL SITES

The Beara Peninsula has numerous sites of archaeological interest. In fact Beara probably has more than any other area of comparable size in Ireland or Europe. These sites, some of which date from 2500 BC, include single standing stones, stone circles, cairns, souter-rains, megalithic tombs, burial grounds, forts, castles, signal towers etc. Consult the Ordnance Survey map of the area (Nos. 84 and 85) to discover many of them.

HEALY PASS

The Healy Pass is a winding mountain road between Adrigole in Co. Cork and Lauragh in Co. Kerry. Cutting through the high Caha Mountains, the Healy Pass rises 334 metres above sea level and passes between two of the highest peaks of the Caha range. This is one of the finest mountain roads in Ireland and is named after Tim Healy, the first Governor-General of the Irish Free State, who was born in nearby Bantry.

DURSEY ISLAND (AND CABLE CAR)

Dursey Island lies off the western extremity of the Beara Peninsula and is connected to the mainland by a cable car, the only one in Ireland. The cable car which carries up to six adults, crosses the treacherous waters of Dursey Sound and operates seven days a week. Cork County Council inaugurated the service in 1969.

COPPER MINING

During the Bronze Age, Beara was probably one of the most important copper mining areas in Europe. In the 19th century copper mining was revived in the area and was concentrated at the western end of the peninsula near Allihies village. The earliest recorded mining here was in 1812, initiated by John Puxley, a landlord, and it finally ceased in the 1960s. Shafts were dug to 450 metres and up to 1,000 people were employed. Today little evidence of the industrial complex around Allihies can be seen but some chimneys, machinery sheds, shaft entrances and spoil heaps are visible. The beach at Ballydonegan outside Allihies village contains tons of sand spoil from the mining.

The BEARA WAY

The Beara Way is a long-distance walking route of 208 km that wends its way through the peninsula. Using tracks, old roads and mountain paths, it takes in some of the most breathtaking scenery in Ireland. It has no official beginning or ending and one can walk sections by following the easily recognised marking posts or a map. It provides a delightful and easy way to discover and explore the peninsula.

CASTLETOWNBERE

French emigre Jaques Fontaine briefly established a Huguenot settlement near Castletownbere in the early years of the18th century. Nearby Bere Island was a British naval station until 1938 and there are remains of naval fortifications still there.

Healy Pass, Beara Peninsula

Seascape, Beara Peninsula

PLACES OF INTEREST

- Archaeological Sites
- Beara Way
- Bere Island
- Dursey Island and Cable Car
- Garinish Island and Gardens
- Healy Pass
- Hungry Hill
- Woods at Glengarriff

Book: *Beara, A Journey Through History*
by Daniel M. O'Brien,
Published by the Beara Hist. Soc.

Mountain stream, Beara Peninsula

Dinish Island and Castletownbere

Sheltering inside Bere Island at the western end of Bantry Bay, Castletownbere is now primarily a fishing port. It is also an RNLI lifeboat station

Cable Car across Dursey Sound

Bull Rock with Lighthouse and large colony of Gannets

CAPE CLEAR
SHERKIN ISLAND
and
BALTIMORE

Old lighthouse on Cape Clear

Take a short ferry trip to the birdwatching island of Cape Clear, known for many rare bird species. The island is familiar to mariners as a conspicuous landmark and was the last outpost of Ireland glimpsed by many emigrants as they sailed for America. On Cape Clear they say that "Ireland is an island off Cape Clear".

Cape Clear is the principal of a cluster of islands in Roaringwater Bay, affectionately known as Carbery's Hundred Isles. It is sometimes referred to as the Queen of Carbery's Hundred Isles.

Cape Clear Island lies 14km off the coast of West Cork and is the most southerly inhabited part of Ireland. The Fastnet Rock lies 6km to the south-west of Cape and is the most southerly point of Ireland. Cape Clear Island is 5km long, 2km wide at its broadest and consists of around 1,500 acres of land. Today, Cape Clear has a population of under 200: before the Famine of the 1840s it numbered more than 1,000. The island is the traditional seat of the O'Driscoll clan.

The climate on Cape Clear is mild, frost and snow being extremely rare in winter. The island gets little shelter from the winds and weather sweeping in from the broad Atlantic Ocean.

The scenery on Cape Clear is wild and beautiful with fine views of the nearby Fastnet Rock, coastline of West Cork and the Atlantic Ocean.

The Gaeltacht is the name given to several areas of Ireland where Irish is the spoken language and many old Irish traditions survive. Cape Clear is in the Gaeltacht and the Irish language is spoken by native islanders. While Irish is their first language, they also speak English. Each summer a large number of students visit the island to learn the Irish language. In the Irish language Cape Clear Island is known as Oilean Chleire.

SAINT CIARAN

St. Ciaran or Kieran was born on Cape Clear around 350 AD. He was the first Irish-born saint and brought Christianity to the region long before St. Patrick's mission elsewhere in Ireland. Not far from the harbour is St. Ciaran's Well and the ruins of the 12th century St. Ciaran's Church, on the site of his early founding. The ferry boat is called the *Naomh Ciaran II* (St. Ciaran). The Christian name Ciaran or Kieran is popular on the island.

Bird Observatory on Cape Clear

FERRY to CAPE CLEAR

The ferry boat (mail boat) *Naomh Ciaran II* sails throughout the year from the mainland harbour of Baltimore to Cape Clear; it takes 45 minutes and travels through Roaringwater Bay, passing many islands and beautiful scenery en route.

In summer other ferry boats travel from Schull on the Mizen Peninsula.

LIGHTHOUSE

The lighthouse (in ruins) lies on the south side of the island. Built in 1818, it was in use until 1854. It was not very successful and several ships were lost in the area. Standing 140m above the sea, it was too high and the light could not be seen in foggy weather. In 1847 the American liner *Stephen Whitney* foundered on the West Calf Island with the loss of 90 lives.

The Fastnet Rock lighthouse replaced this light.

MARINE WILDLIFE

Cape Clear is one of the best places in Ireland to observe whales and dolphins. In late summer many species swim close to the island including Pilot Whale, Porpoise and Common Dolphin: the Bill of Clear is a good viewing point.

Grey Seals are very common around Cape Clear and may be spotted at any time of year.

In summer you may see Leather-back Turtles swimming close to the island. Also, some species of jellyfish.

WILDFLOWERS

Cape Clear has an abundance of wildflowers. Each summer the island is brightly coloured with many species including Bird's-foot Trefoil, Foxglove and Sea Pink.

SHERKIN ISLAND

Sherkin Island is separated from Cape Clear by the Gaskanane Sound, a stretch of water with very strong tides, and a very heavy sea in high winds. Sherkin is about 3km across the sheltered waters of Baltimore harbour from Baltimore pier. A ferry boat links (10 min. trip) Sherkin with Baltimore.

The island is about 5km in length from east to west and 2km in breadth. With less than 100 inhabitants, the population is well down on the 1,000 or so who lived there before the Famine.

Close to Sherkin pier are the extensive ruins of Sherkin Abbey (Franciscan) founded around 1460. The ruins of an O'Driscoll castle stands nearby. Sherkin is a pleasant island to visit for walking and has beautiful sandy beaches, including Silver Strand.

Sherkin Island and Harbour

CAPE CLEAR BIRD OBSERVATORY

Cape Clear Island Bird Observatory is well known internationally by ornithologists who visit each year. The island is recognised as a superb venue for bird-watching because birds can be observed easily at close quarters. In spring and autumn migrating bird species visit the island. Many arrive accidentally and often include birds rare to Ireland of European, American or Asian origin. Cape Clear is known for nesting and migrating seabirds. In foggy conditions or in strong south-west gales, many seabirds can be seen.

Cape Clear Island

BALTIMORE

Baltimore is a picturesque fishing village and sailing centre 13km from Skibbereen, at the mouth of the River Ilen. Historically it was a stronghold of the O'Driscoll clan. In 1537 the men of Waterford, in revenge for an attack made on shipping by Fineen O'Driscoll and his son, landed and set fire to the castle and Baltimore. In 1631 the village was plundered by Algerians who carried off 200 English settlers to captivity in North Africa. After these two calamities Baltimore never regained its former prosperity. Baltimore is often host to visiting yachts from many countries as well as being a successful fishing port, sailing centre, RNLI lifeboat base and gateway to Roaringwater Bay and the islands of Cape Clear and Sherkin.

North Harbour, Cape Clear Island

Sunset at Baltimore

CASTLETOWNSHEND

Castletownshend village is situated on the coast about 8km from Skibbereen. The village developed around the castle which was built in the mid 1600s by the Townshends and is the seat of the family. The steeply-inclined main street runs down to the castle, the quayside and the harbour.
The first castle was built by the O'Driscolls, south of the village, to protect the harbour, and the O'Donovans built a castle on the east side of the harbour.

Castle and Church at Castletownshend

Tower at Castletownshend

The village sits on the north side of Castlehaven Harbour in the parish of Castlehaven, which owes its name to the castle that protects the haven. Anciently it was called Glanbarrahane, named from a deep rocky glen dedicated to St. Barrahane, a local 5th century hermit saint.

A unique feature of Castletownshend is the two sycamore trees growing in the roundabout in the centre of the village. The present sycamores replace two trees planted in the 1800s.

VILLAGE CHURCH

Saint Barrahane's Church (Church of Ireland) stands on a hill overlooking the village close to the castle. It contains beautiful stained glass windows and many historic relics and memorials to the families of the village. Of particular note are three large stone tablets which tell the history of the founding families, many of whose members are buried in the graveyard attached to the church.

SOMERVILLE and ROSS

Somerville and Ross were the pseudonyms of cousins Dr. Edith Somerville (1858 - 1949) and Violet Florence Martin, pen name Martin Ross (1862 - 1915), who wrote a series of humorous novels and short stories. Most of their books were set in a background of West Cork at the turn of the century and told of the experiences of an Irish Resident Magistrate. Their best-known writings were first published in 1928 under the title *The Irish R.M. Complete* and later *Experiences of an Irish R.M.*
The Irish R.M. and *The Real Charlotte* were serialised for television in the 1980s.

During their life together the cousins resided at Drishane House on the outskirts of Castletownshend village. Violet Martin died in 1915 from the effects of a riding accident some years earlier. Edith Somerville continued to live at Drishane between her travels abroad until her death in 1949 at an advanced age. Somerville and Ross are buried in the graveyard at the rear of St. Barrahane's Church, marked by two simple headstones. In the church is the organ Dr. Somerville played for many decades.

PLACES OF INTEREST
- Castletownshend Harbour
- Village Church
- Somerville and Ross Graves
- Toe Head

CLONAKILTY

Clonakilty is an exceptionally attractive town with traditional shop fronts and hand-painted signs. A major town in West Cork, it is a thriving tourist centre. One of its loveliest features is the 18th-century Emmet Square, which is surrounded by stately three-storeyed buildings complete with Georgian doorways.

Clonakilty is a town with an historic background and is first mentioned in records in 1605. In 1613, Sir Richard Boyle, the first Earl of Cork, obtained for the inhabitants a charter of incorporation from James I of England. Under the charter, Sir Richard was constituted lord of the town and supervised the affairs of the corporation.

The charter also conferred the right to send two members to the Irish Parliament, until the union in 1801.

In the early 19th century, the town had a large and prosperous linen manufacturing industry with 400 looms employing 1,000 people. Around the same time up to 40 looms manufactured cotton.

A linen hall (now a bakery) was built and all cloth was brought there to be measured and marked. Corn was shipped from the small port and coal imported on the return journey. However, the harbour was only fit for small vessels, the channel being extremely narrow and dangerous.

CLONAKILTY POST OFFICE

Clonakilty Post Office is unique in Ireland as it was once a Presbyterian church.

Clonakilty Post Office

TRADITIONAL SHOP FRONTS

In Clonakilty town, modern plastic signs and displays have been replaced with traditional wooden shop fronts and a wide variety of hand-painted signs. All of this work is by local crafts people and includes many signs in the Irish language.

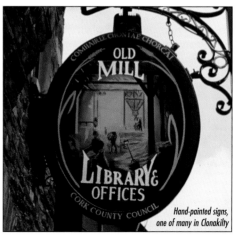

Hand-painted signs, one of many in Clonakilty

Inchydoney Beach

MODEL VILLAGE

The Model Village is the first of its kind in Ireland, containing numerous miniature buildings of architectural and historical interest from the West Cork region. These models have been constructed with great care and attention to detail.

Alongside and part of the centre is a reconstruction of an Irish railway station of the 1940s with many genuine items from that era.

BEACHES

Traditionally Clonakilty is known as the 'Beach Centre of West Cork'. Fine sandy beaches in the Clonakilty region include Inchydoney, Ownahincha, Long Strand and Red Strand. Most beaches have excellent water quality and many have been awarded the International Blue Flag.

Old mill, now
Clonakilty Library

Galley Head

PLACES OF INTEREST
- Beaches
- Birdwatching
  at Clonakilty Estuary and Inchydoney
- Galley Head
- Model Village
- Woodfield,
  birthplace of Gen. Michael Collins

Hand pump, Clonakilty.

DRIMOLEAGUE DRINAGH *and* DUNMANWAY

DRIMOLEAGUE

Built on a tributary of the Ilen River, the village of Drimoleague is situated between the towns of Bantry and Dunmanway. It is one of the few villages in West Cork not close to the sea.

In a pass between two mountains to the north of Drimoleague stand the lofty remains of Castle Donovan. This square tower structure was erected by the head of the clan in the reign of Henry IV and is the ancient seat of the family. It was attacked in 1650 by Cromwellan forces and has remained unoccupied since that time.

DRINAGH

Drinagh village is located east of Drimoleague in central West Cork amid gentle rolling countryside.

Agriculture is the main industry in the area and the village is the headquarters of Drinagh Co-operative, the largest in West Cork. All around, the dairy herds graze the lush, rich green pastures.

DUNMANWAY

The market town of Dunmanway lies on the road between Bantry and Cork city. It is surrounded by hills and rocky mountains to the north, west and south and level ground to the east. The area is well endowed with small lakes and woodlands and is an ideal place for walking.

Historically Dunmanway was ruled by the McCarthys who had a castle in the town and another nearby in Togher. The McCarthys were deposed in 1691 and a colony from England was established by Sir Richard Cox. The market town owes its origins to Sir Richard Cox, Lord Chancellor of Ireland in the reign of William III, who obtained from the king the right to hold a market and fairs. He built the long bridge with its six arches across the Bandon River on the eastern side of the town, and also introduced linen manufacture to the area which flourished in the mid 1700s.

A few miles north of Dunmanway off the Macroom road is the birthplace of Sam Maguire, whose name is inscribed on the All Ireland Gaelic Football Trophy . He was born to a farming family in 1879 and went to work in London in the Civil Service. He was active in the GAA in London and during the struggle for Irish Independence was Director of Intelligence in Britain for the IRA. After independence Maguire came back to Ireland and took a position in the new Irish Civil Service. He eventually returned to his native Dunmanway where he died and is buried in the grave-yard of St. Mary's Church of Ireland.

Lush green pastures near Drimoleague

Purple Loosestrife

Mute Swan

Curraaghlickey Lake, Drinagh

21

The
FASTNET ROCK

Fastnet Rock is one of the most famous landmarks in West Cork and the south-west coast of Ireland. Fastnet lighthouse is well known to mariners as it is the principal landfall light on the south-west coast and is probably the best known around the Irish and British coasts. Fastnet Rock lies out in the Atlantic Ocean, 6km south-west of Cape Clear Island. It is the most southerly point in Ireland and consists of a jagged pinnacle of hard clay-slate rock, surrounded by deep water on all sides. Strong currents circle the rock and the water is rarely calm enough to allow landing directly from a boat, except in very calm conditions. It is locally known as 'Ireland's Teardrop', as Fastnet Rock was one of the last parts of Ireland seen by Irish emigrants as they sailed to America.

FASTNET ROCK LIGHTHOUSE

One of the first lighthouses in the s.w. region was built on Cape Clear Island in 1818. However, the light was too high and was not visible to ships in foggy weather. In 1847 the American liner *Stephen Whitney* with 110 passengers and crew foundered on the West Calf Island. Ninety lives were lost including the captain. After this mishap it was decided to move the light to the nearby Fastnet Rock.

The first Fastnet lighthouse was built in 1853 and was constructed of cast iron. A light shone for the first time on January 1st 1854. It was one of the first oil-burning lights in these islands and was 38,000 candle power: today's light is 1.3 million candle power. This lighthouse was designed by George Halpin, who designed many of the lighthouses around Ireland and Britain at the time, and cost £17,390 to build.

However, cast-iron lighthouses were found to be unsafe — a similar lighthouse on the Calf Rock, to the west near the Bull Rock, was demolished in a storm. Towards the end of the 19th century it was apparent that the Fastnet light was not sufficiently powerful for its critical position and should be improved, so the authorities decided to construct the present lighthouse.

The granite for its construction was shipped from Penryn in Cornwall to a specially constructed stone yard at Rock Island near Crookhaven on the Mizen Peninsula. A total of 2,074 granite blocks, in 89 courses from foundation to top, were used.

Preparations for construction commenced in 1897. Taking five years to complete, the first block was set in June 1899 and the last in June 1904. All materials were transported to the Fastnet from Rock Island on the steamer *Ierne* which was especially built for the project. The lighthouse cost almost £90,000 to construct and the present light shone for the first time on June 24th 1904.

The light is now automatic and the last lighthouse keeper left the Fastnet in 1989.

FASTNET YACHT RACE

The Fastnet Yacht Race is held in August every other year. The route is from Cowes, Isle of Wight, south of England around the Fastnet Rock and back to Plymouth in Devon, a distance of 1,000 km. The race was first held in 1925 and since 1957 it has been the final race of the Admiral's Cup competition.

BOAT TRIPS

Boat trips around the Fastnet Rock operate from Cape Clear Island and Schull Harbour in summer. For details inquire locally at Baltimore, Cape Clear and Schull.

Book: *History of the Fastnet Rock Lighthouse* by C. W. Scott. Re-issued in 1993, by Schull Books, Co. Cork.

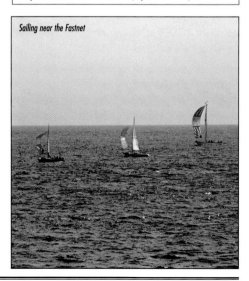
Sailing near the Fastnet

Fastnet Rock and Lighthouse

GLENGARRIFF

Glengarriff, surrrounded by Oak Woods.

The lovely village of Glengarriff has for many years been a popular and renowned holiday resort. Glengarriff nestles in a glen in the midst of rocks, cliffs and mountains, at the head of a tiny inlet, in the north-eastern corner of Bantry Bay.

It derives its name from the Irish Gleann Garbh 'rough glen' and is an area of great scenic beauty. The glen is the result of glacial deepening during the last Ice Age 10,000 years ago. There are many signs of glacial activity in the area, including a large number of rocks deposited on the mountainside by moving ice, and lines in the rocks showing which direction the ice moved.

The climate of the area is very mild due to the Gulf Stream. However, the high mountains prompt the moist south-westerly winds to deposit a great deal of rainfall, up to 2000mm per annum in some places.

Autumn in Glengarriff Wood

HISTORY

Glengarriff has strong associations with the O'Sullivans, the former chieftains or princes of Beare. In 1602, after the battle of Kinsale, the remnants of the O'Sullivan clan departed from Glengarriff on their Long March to Leitrim, over 300 km in 15 days, to join the O'Rourke clan.

BRIDGE

Glengarriff is the gateway to the beautiful Beara Peninsula and historically has always been an important river crossing. On crossing the present bridge leading from Glengarriff to Castletownbere, to the left of the road beyond the old bridge you can see an ancient bridge known as Cromwell's Bridge. In fact the bridge probably predates Cromwell and was in use until the early 1800s.

GARINISH ISLAND or ILNACULLIN

Garinish Island Garden is a place of rare beauty, set in a fifteen-hectare island in the sheltered harbour of Glengarriff, Bantry Bay. Garinish Island is also called Ilnacullin and should not be confused with Garnish Island Gardens in Co. Kerry.

Ilnacullin (meaning island of holly) is well known to horticulturists and lovers of trees and shrubs the world over.

The most attractive feature of Garinish is the Italian-style garden comprising a rectangular lily-pond surrounded by paved walks with two classical pavilions, the Casita and Medici House, at each end.

The island was windswept and barren when it was purchased by Annan Bryce in 1910. He commissioned Harold Peto, a noted landscape architect at the time, to draw up plans to transform it into a place of beauty. In 1953, on the death of Annan Bryce's son Rowland, Garinish Island was bequeathed to the Irish nation and since then the Commissioners of Public Works has been entrusted to continue the process of development.

Garinish can be reached by a short boat journey from Glengarriff. Other attractions on Garinish include the Martello tower built in the early 1800s, the Common Seals basking on the rocky shore as the boats pass and the fine views of the mountain scenery of West Cork.

Fungi growing on trees

SEALS

Fine views of the Common Seals basking on the rocky shore may be had as the boats pass by. Despite their name, Common Seals are scarce in Ireland and this is the only colony on the south coast.

Common Seal on the rocks near Garinish Island

GLENGARRIFF WOOD

Glengarriff Wood is a National Nature Reserve containing about 300 hectares owned and managed by the National Parks and Wildlife Service. The main entrance to Glengarriff Wood is via the old lodge gate, 1.5km north of Glengarriff on the Kenmare road (N71). Located at the end of a glacially deepened valley, the wood is the remnant of a once very extensive native oakwood. The wood is an example of oceanic Sessile Oak woodland, rated as second only in importance to the Killarney Oakwoods. Glengarriff Wood is composed mainly of Sessile Oak, Holly, Birch and Rowan. Other tree species include Alder, Ash, Sycamore, Scots Pine, Strawberry Tree, Willow, Yew and the Rhododendron shrub.Glengarriff Wood is a comfortable place for walking with signposts to guide. The Beara Way route also passes through the area.

PLACES OF INTEREST

- Bantry Bay
- Garinish Island and Gardens
- Barley Lake
- Glengarriff Woods

Rhododendron ponticum

BIRDS

Many species of woodland birds are to be seen at Glengarriff Wood including Blackbird, Chaffinch, Coal Tit and Jay. A colourful member of the Crow family, the Jay is rare in Ireland but frequently seen in the wood.

BUTTERFLIES

There are many species of butterfly in Glengarriff Wood including Orange Tip, Painted Lady, Speckled Wood, Green-veined White, Holly Blue and Purple Hairstreak.

Painted Lady

The STRAWBERRY TREE

The Strawberry Tree (*Arbutus unedo*) is so named because of its red strawberry-like fruits, which take one whole year to ripen and appear alongside the cream-coloured flowers in October. Holly and the Strawberry Tree are Ireland's only native evergreen, broadleaf trees.

Found mainly along the Mediterranean, it is rare in Ireland. Glengarriff Wood is one of the few places in Ireland where the Strawberry Tree grows.

Strawberry Tree

Wood Sorrel

TUNNELS

On the N71 from Glengarriff to Kenmare one passes through a series of small tunnels at the Cork/Kerry border. Construction commenced in July 1833 from plans prepared by William Bald. The spectacular scenery in the area includes views of Bantry Bay and the Atlantic Ocean.

One of the many waterfalls near Glengarriff

GOUGANE BARRA

Source of the River Lee at Gougane Barra

Gougane Barra is surrounded by the lofty mountains of the Cork and Kerry chain and is one of the most scenic places in West Cork.
Numerous streams descend from the mountains, forming cascades which constantly supply the lake at Gougane Barra.
Historically, Gougane Barra was part of the territory of the O'Learys which the clan lost following the Cromwellian Wars. Subsequently the lands passed to the London Guilds and Companies, the Townshend family, and in the early part of this century to farming tenants.

SAINT FINBAR

Finbar is traditionally associated with Gougane Barra. He was born near Bandon in 560 AD and upon completion of his priestly training arrived in Gougane Barra to found his first monastery on the island in the lake. It is probable that the buildings were of timber, which have long disappeared.

The present stone court with its eight cells was erected about 1700 by Rev. Denis O'Mahony who, following in the footsteps of Finbar, lived here for 30 years in solitude. His burial place near the island is marked.

MODERN ORATORY

The present oratory was built about 1900. Constructed from local sandstone, it has a carved head of Saint Finbar inserted above the doorway.

Forest Park at Gougane Barra

GOUGANE BARRA LAKE

Gougane Barra Lake lies near the source of the River Lee, one of Cork's major rivers. Cork city is built on the River Lee. The river supplies drinking water to the city and generates electricity.

GOUGANE BARRA FOREST

Up to 1938, Gougane Barra was a bare valley. In that year the Forest Service planted the first coniferous trees and since then Gougane Barra has been maturing into an attractive woodland. It is one of a few forests with a motor trail.

WOODLAND BIRDS

Birds you may see in Gougane Barra woods include the Blackbird, Coal Tit, Wren and Wood Pigeon.

PLACES OF INTEREST
● Gougane Barra Oratory
● Lake ● Woodlands

WALKING

Walking in Gougane Barra is a very rewarding experience. From the car park there are many walks but the two most popular are the ring walk and the nature trail.

Gougane Barra Oratory

LOUGH HYNE

Lough Hyne

Visit a beautiful nature reserve and enjoy some of the finest scenery in West Cork.
Situated on the coast between Skibbereen and Baltimore, Lough Hyne is a saline marine lough or sea-lough and is a notable landmark in West Cork. The salt water enters from the open Atlantic Ocean through Barloge Creek and the Rapids. Lough Hyne is one of the few sea-loughs in Ireland. The lough has no significant rivers except for a few very small streams which flow from the small catchment area after rainfall.
The name Hyne and Ine are both used and it is thought the name derives from the Irish loch dhoimhin (deep lake), from a belief that the lough is bottomless.
Lough Hyne is roughly rectangular in shape, measuring 1km by 3/4 km and almost 55 metres deep. It is sheltered from winds by the surrounding hills.
In the centre of the lough, the ruins of Cloghan Castle stand on Castle Island. The castle was built by the O'Driscoll clan to protect the entrance to the lough from the sea.

MARINE NATURE RESERVE

Lough Hyne is of immense scientific importance as well as being an area of great natural beauty. In 1981 Lough Hyne became Ireland's first Marine Nature Reserve. It was established to protect the treasure trove of marine life. The nature reserve also includes the Rapids and Barloge Creek.

MARINE LIFE

For its size Lough Hyne contains a wider range of marine species than any other place in Ireland. The lough contains a wide variety of marine habitats in a small sheltered area and consequently it has a great diversity of marine animals and plants. Marine animals of special interest include the Purple Sea Urchin *(Paracentrotus lividus)*, which grazes on the algae on rocks in shallow water. If you look into the shallow waters of the lough near the car park, you may see this dark-purple Sea Urchin.

The Red Mouth Goby is a small fish of Mediterranean distribution. Lough Hyne is one of the few places in Ireland where it is found. The lough abounds with many more marine species including numerous colourful Sea Anemones and rare Algae. Lough Hyne is noted for the variety of Sea Slug species in its waters.

RAPIDS and BARLOGE CREEK

The Rapids lie between Lough Hyne and Barloge Creek, and consist of a narrow rocky channel through which the tide pours in and out at speeds approaching ten miles per hour. Although dangerous to swimmers, the strong currents support an extraordinary rich marine life of multi-coloured Sponges, Sea Squirts, Sea Anemones and Starfish, all growing underneath a dense canopy of kelp.

KNOCKOMAGH HILL and WOOD

Explore wooded Knockomagh Hill, where the trees part occasionally to offer tantalising glimpses of Lough Hyne and the surrounding countryside. Knockomagh Hill (197 metres) is the highest point in the immediate vicinity of Lough Hyne. The climb to the summit is steep and testing but is well worthwhile for the magnificent views of the Lough, rugged coastline, Atlantic Ocean, the distant Stag Rocks, Galley Head, Cape Clear, Sherkin Island, and Roaringwater Bay. Bring your camera!

A) *Lough Hyne and Barloge Creek*
B) *Woodland path at Knockomagh Hill*
C) *Purple Sea Urchin (Paracentrotus lividus)*
D) *Black Goby*

A) Rapids at Barloge Creek
B) Snake Pipefish
C) Shrimp
D) Jewel Anemone
E) Sea Slug feeding on Sea Mat
F) Red-Mouth Goby
G) Tompot Blenny

ISLANDS
of
WEST CORK

The long West Cork coastline is dotted with islands and rocks. Many islands were once inhabited but now abandoned, while others have only a small number of residents today.

The seven inhabited islands in West Cork are Bere, Whiddy (Bantry Bay), Cape Clear, Hare, Long, Sherkin (Roaringwater Bay) and Dursey at the end of the Beara Peninsula. Islands no longer inhabited include the Calf Isles., Castle, Horse and Skeam Isles. Islands are fascinating places to visit.

C O U

DURSEY ISLAND

Dursey Island lies off the western extremity of the Beara Peninsula. It is the only island in Ireland with a cable car connection to the mainland. The island is two and a half kilometres long, one kilometre wide and comprises some 1,500 acres of rugged terrain and pasture land. The island has less than a dozen residents. Between the island and the mainland is a narrow sound: through which vessels pass and the cable car travels overhead.

Book: *Discovering Dursey,* by Penelope Durell, gives much detail about the island.

WHIDDY ISLAND

Situated in Bantry Bay, Whiddy Island has become well known through the oil terminal located there. It has fewer than 50 inhabitants and a regular ferry boat service from Bantry pier.

CAPE CLEAR

Cape Clear lies 15km (9mi) off the sailing and fishing village of Baltimore. It is the only island in Cork where the native inhabitants (over 100) still speak the Irish language. Ferry boats sail from Baltimore throughout the year and from Schull in summer time.

LONG ISLAND

Long Island lies off Schull Harbour in Roaringwater Bay. It is 3 km long and 1 km wide and has under 30 residents. It comprises around 150 acres of land. It is very close to the mainland and does not have a regular ferry service.

HARE ISLAND

Hare is a small island located in the inner part of Roaringwater Bay and has around 20 inhabitants. The ferry boat sails regularly from Cunnamore Point on the mainland to the island.

BERE ISLAND

Bere Island near the mouth of Bantry Bay is one of the largest offshore islands in West Cork. It is 10 km long by 4 km wide and has a population of just over 200, well below the 2,000 prior to the Great Famine in the mid 19th century.

Between the mainland and Bere Island is a stretch of water known as Berehaven Sound. It is well sheltered and is a good deep water anchorage for large ships.

Bere Island has a long association with the military which commenced in 1797, after the arrival of the French fleet in Bantry Bay. The Government of the time erected a signal tower, five Martello towers and a barracks for 150 men on Bere island. Today the island is still used by the Irish military.

The ferryboat sails regularly from the mainland at Castletownbere.

Book: *Bere Island - a Short History,* by Ted O'Sullivan

C O R K

Y CORK

SHERKIN ISLAND

Sherkin Island lies just off Baltimore Harbour. It is about 5km in length from east to west, 2km wide and has fewer than 100 inhabitants. In the past the island was a stronghold of the O'Driscoll clan. The remains of an O'Driscoll castle and a Franciscan monastery are to be seen close to the pier. Silver Strand is one of the finest sandy beaches in West Cork. The ferry boat to the island sails throughout the year from Baltimore harbour.

OFFSHORE ROCKS

Apart from the islands, West Cork has many off-shore rocks such as Bull Rock, the Stags and the Fastnet Rock.

Bull Rock lies off the Beara Peninsula and has a lighthouse which is now unmanned but still in operation through automation. The rock is home to many species of seabirds including Gannet, Guillemot, Razorbill and Shag. It holds the second largest colony of nesting Gannets in Ireland.

The Stag Rocks lie off Toe Head and consist of a series of jagged rocks. Many trawlers and large ships have foundered there over the years. The *Kowloon Bridge* bulk carrier sank in 1986 close to the Stags. Carrying iron ore from Canada to Britain, it got into difficulties in the Atlantic Ocean. A buoy and light now mark the spot to the west of the Stag Rocks.

The Fastnet Rock with its lighthouse is probably the best known of all offshore rocks on the south coast.

KINSALE

Kinsale is one of the oldest towns in County Cork. Situated in the estuary of the River Bandon, it is a place of great antiquity, a market town, sea port and prominent sailing centre.

This picturesque resort is a centre for sea angling, golf and gourmet eating.

OLD HEAD of KINSALE

The headland 10km south of the town is known as the Old Head of Kinsale. It is a well-known landmark to mariners on the south coast and is a nationally important breeding site for seabirds including Guillemot, Razorbill and Kittiwake.

LIGHTHOUSE

The present lighthouse on the Old Head of Kinsale stands beside the ruins of two older lighthouses, one from the 17th century and the other from the 18th.

Entrance to Charles Fort

Sailing Centre in Kinsale Harbour

BATTLE of KINSALE

The Battle of Kinsale in December 1601 between English and Spanish forces was a turning point in Irish history.

The Spanish fleet, aiding the Irish rebellion against English rule, landed at Kinsale in the autumn of 1601. The Spanish forces under the command of Don Juan D'Aquila took possession of Kinsale as the English forces laid siege to the town. The army of Earl O'Neill from Ulster marched on Kinsale to give support to the Spaniards but was routed with great slaughter.

The battle is significant because it was one of the last great battles fought on Irish soil, increasing the exodus of Irish soldiers, churchmen and Gaelic lords to the continent of Europe. This became known as the Flight of the Earls and ended an era of Gaelic society in Ireland.

Razorbills at Kinsale Head

CHARLES FORT

Charles Fort was built in the early 1680s and is named in honour of Charles II, the then reigning monarch. In the 17th century Kinsale was a safe haven for ships and an important trading town. Charles Fort was built on the eastern bank (along with James Fort on the western bank) to protect the town. Star-shaped in design, the fort has zigzag walls to provide cross-fire from several directions against any attacker.

It was occupied by James II (Charles II's successor) in 1690, but was taken by his Williamite opponents, who exploited its one weak spot by firing down from the high ground behind.

BEACHES

There are a number of sandy beaches in the Kinsale area, some with the International Blue Flag Award.

LUSITANIA

The *Lusitania*, a British ocean liner was sunk by a German submarine on May 7th 1915 in sight of the Old Head of Kinsale. Returning from New York to Liverpool, 1,198 out of 1,959 passengers and crew were drowned. The sinking contributed indirectly to the entry of the U.S. into World War 1. A memorial stone is located at the Old Head of Kinsale.

Lusitania Memorial at Kinsale Head

GOURMET CAPITAL of IRELAND

Kinsale is well endowed with many excellent owner-run restaurants and is known as 'the gourmet capital of Ireland'. Local fishermen provide their catch for the fine dishes served in the restaurants.

SAILING

Kinsale with its renowned sailing club is a base frequented by sailing yachts from all over the world.

MACROOM

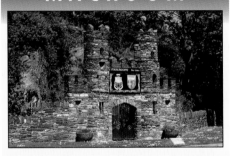

Yellow Flag

Macroom, a thriving market town west of Cork city, is situated in a fertile vale surrounded by low hills on the River Sullane, a tributary of the River Lee. The name Macroom is said to derive from the Irish word for a crooked plain.

The town developed around the castle built by the Carews. The remains of this castle, which had a long and eventful history, can still be seen. It was once occupied by the local Irish chieftains, the McCarthys, and was burned on several occasions.

Inchigeelagh Lakes

Macroom Castle

GEARAGH

The Gearagh is a reservoir on the upper section of the River Lee, situated near Macroom town on the Inchigeelagh road. The name is derived from Gaoire, the Irish word for wooded river. The Gearagh contains the remnants of a once-large alluvial ancient oak forest, now submerged. When the water levels are low, the blackened oak stumps of the old forest are visible. The area has a unique network of branched streams with small islands.

The Gearagh is noted for a rich variety of wildlife. Among its trees are Oak, Birch, Holly and a wealth of ground flora, including ferns and wildflowers. Watch out for the small white flowers of Mudwort *(Limosella aquatica)*, a rare wildflower of muddy shores. In summer the Gearagh teams with dragonflies, while in winter many species of birds can be seen, such as dabbling ducks and Whooper Swans.

Sunset over the Gearagh

Mute Swans swim among the oak tree stumps at the Gearagh

MIZEN PENINSULA

The Mizen Peninsula is a place of great natural beauty. It is surrounded by the clear waters of Dunmanus Bay to the north, the Atlantic Ocean to the west, and Roaringwater Bay to the south. The ocean, miles of coastline, and the rugged landscape all contribute to the magnificent scenery of the Mizen Peninsula.

Mizen is one of three peninsulas in West Cork and stretches from the village of Ballydehob westward for 25km (17 miles), encompassing the villages of Schull, Toormore, Goleen and Crookhaven and ending at Mizen Head.

Durrus village is the gateway from the west to the Mizen Peninsula. From here the road cuts through the middle of the peninsula on to Toormore and then to Crookhaven village and Mizen Head.

The Mizen Peninsula overlooks Roaringwater Bay and its islands, affectionately known as Carbery's Hundred Isles. Several vantage points offer fine views of Cape Clear, Sherkin and Fastnet Rock

Sea angling boats in Schull Harbour

MIZEN HEAD
Mizen Head, the most south-westerly headland in Ireland, is regularly mentioned in weather forecasts and shipping information, and is one of the best-known headlands in Ireland.

Mizen Head, Ireland's most south-westerly point

MIZEN FOG SIGNAL STATION
Mizen Head Fog Signal Station stands at the extremity of the peninsula and came into operation in 1909. The last keepers departed in 1993 and the fog signal station was opened to the public for the first time in 1994.

SCHULL
Schull is a picturesque fishing village nestling between the sea and Mount Gabriel. It is the largest village on the Mizen peninsula and is a well-known centre for sailing, sea angling and tourism. Its narrow streets and old-style shop fronts contribute to its traditional atmosphere.

SCHULL PLANETARIUM
The Planetariun is situated in the grounds of Schull Community College. Sitting under a hemispherical

Mizen Light

dome in a darkened auditorium, spectators can see an amazingly realistic and accurate reproduction of the star-studded night sky. Visitors are welcome.

MARCONI

At the end of the 19th century ships sailed close to Brow Head to announce their arrival and communicate news from America, especially on financial matters. This news was quickly relayed to London and arrived many hours before the ship docked in England. However, it was hazardous for large ships to come so close to land.

A cable was laid between Fastnet Rock and Brow Head to relay the information from Fastnet but the cable snapped continually and it never operated sucessfully. The Italian wireless pioneer Guglielmo Marconi was invited to rectify the problem by installing a wireless. At the beginning of the 1900s Marconi arrived in Crookhaven and opened a wireless station at Brow Head. Ships could now connect directly with Brow Head while staying safely out at sea.

For years the station functioned at Brow Head before moving to Valentia in Kerry. The building at the summit of Brow Head is all that remains.

Mount Gabriel

MOUNT GABRIEL

Mount Gabriel (400 metres high) is one of the most visible landmarks on the Mizen Peninsula. On its summit, the golfball-like structures enclose a radar tracking system for the safe navigation of aircraft in the air corridor overhead.

HISTORICAL SITES

Since ancient times man has lived on the Mizen Peninsula and maybe one of the first parts of Ireland to be inhabited. Mizen has numerous sites of archaeological interest and many date back to pre-Christianity. The sites include ancient copper mines, promontory forts, standing stones, megalithic tombs, ruined castles and churches. These monuments provide a tangible record of the past in this region.

The Bronze Age megalithic tomb at Altar on the eastern side of Toormore Bay is designated a national monument and very easy to visit.

Iron Age coastal promontory forts can be seen at Dooneen, Dunmanus Bay and Three Castle Head.

In the past the Mizen Peninsula was ruled by Irish chieftains including McCarthy, O'Donovan, O'Driscoll and O'Mahony.

A McCarthy castle stands on the seashore at Kilcoe and there are O'Mahony castles at Dunbeacon, Dunmanus, Rossbrin and Three Castle Head. These castles were built in the Medieval Period.

> GUIDE: *The Beautiful Mizen Peninsula* guide/map, contains many colour photographs and information about the Mizen, including Archaeological Sites, Flora and Fauna etc. On sale locally.

Mizen Fog Signal Station

Stormy waters at Mizen

ROSSCARBERY

Rosscarbery is a town with a rich historical background. Set at the head of an inlet on the coast between Clonakilty and Skibbereen, it is in the Barony of East Carbery.

The name Rosscarbery is said to derive from the Irish Ros O'Cairbre, the Wood of the Carberys. In the early part of the 6th century St. Fachtna founded a monastery at Rosscarbery and presided there until his death. The monastery under his successors became a celebrated seat of learning, much used by families from the south-west of Ireland.

Rosscarbery is the seat of the Church of Ireland diocese of Ross. The See of Ross had its origins in the foundation of the monastery by St. Fachtna, the church of which became the cathedral church of the diocese in the 6th century and its founder the first bishop. A 12th century cathedral preceded the present St. Fachtna's, which has a prominent spire.

PLACES OF INTEREST
- Beaches (Long Strand, Ownahincha, Warren)
- Castlefreke
- Coppinger's Court
- Drombeg Stone Circle
- Galley Head

View of historic Rosscarbery across the lagoon

COPPINGER'S COURT
Coppinger's Court is situated between Rosscarbery and Glandore. This Elizabethan-style court house was built in the early years of the 17th century by Sir Walter Coppinger, who settled here after the Battle of Kinsale. It was the centrepiece of what was to be a new development in the area. The building was attacked and burned down during the 1641 rebellion. The ruins stand roofless and contain some characteristic architectural features of the period.

DROMBEG STONE CIRCLE
One of Cork's outstanding archaeological sites is the Bronze Age stone circle at Drombeg, 3km east of Glandore village on the Rosscarbery road. It is one of the finest stone circles in West Cork. Its winter solstice sunset was only noted in the early 1900s.

Ornate entrance to St. Fachtna's Church

RATHBARRY and CASTLEFREKE

East of Rosscarbery on the coast road is Rathbarry, which derives its name from an ancient fort. Rathbarry Castle (in ruins) was erected in the 15th century by Randal Og Barry and was burned during the 1641 rebellion.

Castlefreke mansion (castle type) was built in the late 19th century in a distinctive Gothic style and was seat of the Earls of Carbery. The building was inhabited until the 1950s.

CASTLEFREKE WOODS

Castlefreke is surrounded by a coniferous wood plantation with pleasant woodland walks.

BEACHES

Beautiful sandy beaches at the Long Strand, Ownahincha and the Warren.

Ferns and mosses at Castlefreke woods

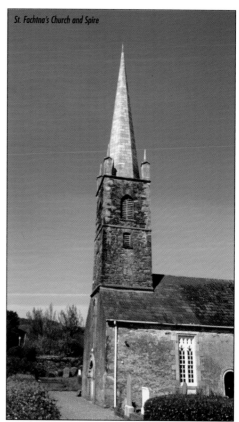

St. Fachtna's Church and Spire

The Warren Beach

SHEEP'S HEAD PENINSULA

Sheep's Head

Light at tip of Sheep's Head

The Sheep's Head Peninsula lies between the waters of Bantry Bay (north) and Dunmanus Bay (south). Between Beara and Mizen, it is the smallest of the three peninsulas in West Cork.

The Irish name for the Sheep's Head Peninsula is Muintir Bhaire. It is believed that Baire was a member of the Corca Luighe, the race of Lughaidh. It is not known exactly how the name Sheep's Head derived.

VILLAGES

The villages of Ahakista, Durrus and Kilcrohane are the main centres of population on the Sheep's Head Peninsula.

Átha an Chist
AHAKISTA

Evening at Dunmanus Bay

Tranquil waters of Dunmanus Bay

PLACES OF INTEREST
- Air India Disaster Memorial
- Sheep's Head Beacon Light
- Sheep's Head Way
- Views of Bantry and Dunmanus Bays

BEACON
The small white building at the very tip of the Sheep's Head Peninsula contains a navigation light to guide vessels entering and leaving Bantry Bay.

SHEEP'S HEAD WAY
The Sheep's Head Way is a loop walk of about 90km taking in the Sheep's Head Peninsula and the general Bantry area.

GOAT'S PATH ROAD
The road on the north shore of the Sheep's Head Peninsula, from Bantry through Gerahies, is known as the Goat's Path. From this road there are impressive views of Bantry Bay and Whiddy Island.

AIR INDIA DISASTER MEMORIAL
The memorial sundial, close to the water's edge near Ahakista, was erected in memory of the 331 people who died in the Air India plane explosion 300km out in the Atlantic on June 23rd 1985.

Sea Pink

Air India disaster memorial near Ahakista

SKIBBEREEN

Skibbereen is situated on the River Ilen in the heart of West Cork in an area of great scenic beauty. It is a busy market town and considered by many as the major centre of West Cork. This is an attractive town where colourful buildings and traditional shop fronts blend in harmony with modern commerce.
The town is the location of St. Patrick's cathedral church of the small Roman Catholic diocese of Ross

HISTORY

Up to 1600 most of the land around Skibbereen belonged to the native McCarthy clan. A major reason for Skibbereen's development was the raid on the neighbouring seaport of Baltimore in 1631 (Sack of Baltimore) by Algerian pirates. Many people were killed, while others were taken away: consequently the remaining inhabitants moved up river to the safety of Skibbereen, a small trading centre at the time. In the early 1800s Skibbereen was noted for woollen and linen manufacture, while today its economic activities are agriculture, fishing, food production and tourism.

The GREAT FAMINE

Skibbereen town and its environs were greatly affected by the Great Famine of the 1840s. With the failure of the potato crop, their staple food, many thousands of the local population starved or died from famine-related diseases. Many victims were buried in a communal grave in the local Abbey cemetery: the visitor can still see this famine plot. Thousands of people from the area emigrated all over the world.

MAID OF ERIN

The Maid of Erin statue is a local landmark situated in the town square. It was erected in 1904 by the local committee of the Young Ireland Society to commemorate the Irish Rebellions of 1798, 1803, 1848 and 1867.

SKIBBEREEN EAGLE

"It will keep its eye on the Emperor of Russia and all such despotic enemies - whether at home or abroad" This somewhat grandiose statement of editorial policy which appeared in the *Skibbereen Eagle* on September 5th 1898, became accepted as the newspaper's very own prerogative or claim. Ever since, 'Keeping an Eye on Russia" has been frequently quoted in newspapers throughout the English speaking world as well as on radio and television. Today the *Southern Star,* successor to the *Skibbereen Eagle,* continues to keep its readers informed.

FAMOUS PEOPLE

The Irish patriot Jeremiah O'Donovan-Rossa, born near Rosscarbery, was employed for many years in the centre of Skibbereen before emigrating to America. General Michael Collins departed from the Eldon Hotel to his death at the ambush in Beal na Blath in 1922. Edith Somerville and Violet Ross, authors of the humorous *Irish R.M.* resided at nearby Castletownshend. They are buried in the cemetery attached to the church in the village.

PLACES OF INTEREST
- Baltimore, Cape Clear and Sherkin Island
- Castletownshend
- Famine Plot (at Abbey Cemetery)
- Lough Hyne ● Mizen Head
- Schull Planetarium

TIMOLEAGUE
and
COURTMACSHERRY

Timoleague village lies east of Clonakilty on the Argideen estuary and derives its name from the Irish Tig Mologa, house of St. Mologa. Timoleague Franciscan Abbey is dedicated to St. Mologa and was built in 1312 possibly by McCarthy, the local chieftain.

Birdsfoot Trefoil

Courtmacsherry is a maritime village 4 km south east from Timoleague and is pleasantly situated in the harbour of the same name. It is a sea angling centre and the home station of a RNLI lifeboat. Courtmacsherry Bay and Timoleague Estuary host many interesting species of wild birds.

Timoleague with its Abbey

UNION HALL
GLANDORE
and LEAP

Union Hall

UNION HALL
Union Hall lies across from Glandore on the western side of Glandore Harbour. It is a lively fishing port and one of the most important on the south coast of Ireland.

LEAP
Leap, is a small village at the northern end of Glandore Harbour and divides East Carbery from West Carbery. The name commemorates a local chieftain allegedly jumping across the steep gorge while being pursued.

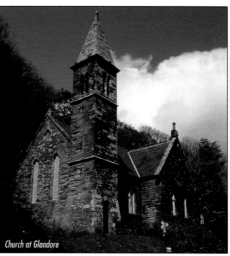
Church at Glandore

GLANDORE
Glandore village is 5km west of Rosscarbery overlooking beautiful Glandore harbour. The tranquil harbour is often host to yachts from many nations, cruising the south coast of Ireland.

The scenery of Glandore and nearby Myross is extremely picturesque and was the subject of a Latin poem, *Carberiae Rupes*, written by Dean Swift who spent some time in the region. Glandore must have been a significant place at an early period, judging by the presence of castles at Glandore and Kilfinnan.

Peaceful waters at Glandore Harbour

ARCHAEOLOGICAL SITES

Archaeological sites abound in West Cork.
An archaeological inventory of West Cork compiled
by the Office of Public Works records almost 4,000
in all, the greatest density anywhere in Europe.
Some sites contain monuments dating back
to pre-Christian times and include megalithic wedge
tombs, stone circles, standing stones and ringforts.

These sites record the colonisation of West Cork
by man and include monuments dating from
the Neolithic Period 4000 BC,
Bronze Age 2000 BC,
Iron Age 500 BC,
Early Christian Period 500 AD
and the Medieval Period from 1000 AD.

The location of many archaeological sites can be
found by referring to the Ordnance Survey maps
(Discovery Series), numbers 84 to 89.
Most archaeological sites in West Cork are on
private property, seek permission from the
land owner before you visit.

The local Historical and Archaeological Societies of
Beara and Mizen regularly lead guided outings
to historical sites in the area.
Visitors are welcome to join them on their outings:
see locally for details.

Two fine examples of West Cork archaeological
monuments are Drombeg Stone Circle, near
Glandore and the Megalithic Tomb at Altar on the
eastern side of Toormore Bay.

STANDING STONES and STONE CIRCLES

Single upright stones are a common feature in West Cork. Over 300 have been recorded in the area and probably date to the Bronze Age. Some mark prehistoric burials, while others may have had a ritual use as they appear to have a north-east/south-west axis.

Stone circles consist of a ring of free-standing stones. The circle is uneven in number and arranged so that the axial stone is set directly opposite the two tallest stones which mark the entrance to the circle.

Stone circles are divided into two groups, five-stone or multi-stone circles, and were used as ritual sites where ceremonies took place. No one knows the exact date but they are likely to be Bronze Age.

Standing stone at Rosscarbery

DROMBEG STONE CIRCLE

Drombeg Stone Circle is located in a pasture between the village of Glandore and Rosscarbery.

It is a multiple-stone circle consisting of seventeen stones, two missing and one fallen. It seems to be aligned north-east/south-west and during the winter solstice the sun appears to set on a point of the horizon in line with the axis of the circle.

The site was excavated in 1957 and five pits were found within the circle; one contained a deposit of cremated human bone which was radiocarbon-dated to be from about 600 AD.

Drombeg Stone Circle is easy to visit, follow the sign-posts.

Wedge Tomb at Altar, near Toormore.

*For more information consult
"Archaeological Inventory of County Cork,
Vol 1, West Cork" by the Office of Public Works.*

MEGALITHIC TOMB at ALTAR

The Megalithic Tomb at Altar near Toormore (7km west of Schull village on the seaward side of the road) is in very good condition.

Locally known as 'Altar', it is easily accessible and is said to have been used as a mass rock in the past. It is open to the public, signposted, and has a car park.

MEGALITHIC TOMBS

Throughout the Neolithic and Early Bronze Age c.3500 - 1500 BC farming communities over much of western Europe including Ireland buried their dead in the collective burial chambers of stone now known as Megalithic Tombs. The tomb, generally wedge-shaped, consists of a burial chamber with a wall of large upright stones and roofed over with a lintel of stone. Originally the tomb was contained within a mound of stones (cairn) with access at one end of the chamber. The dead were placed within the chamber and often accompanied by pottery or arrow heads. Forty tombs, mostly wedge shaped, have been discovered in West Cork, all in coastal locations and facing in a south-westerly direction.

HISTORICAL SITES

Coppinger's Court near Glandore

West Cork is rich in historical sites. Some coastal promontory forts date back to the Iron Age (about 350 BC), with good examples at Three Castle Head and Dooneen on Dunmanus Bay.

There are a number of castles (in ruins) in West Cork from the Medieval Period. These include the O'Mahony castles at Dunbeacon, Dunmanus, Rossbrin and Three Castle Head, and a McCarthy castle stands on the seashore at Kilcoe.

Franciscan Abbey at Sherkin Island

Many historic sites are situated on private lands, so seek permission before entering.

Martello Tower, Beara

Castles beside lake on Tree Castle Head

MARTELLO and SIGNAL TOWERS

After the attempted French invasion of Bantry Bay in 1796, a number of Martello towers (round) were constructed on the islands of Bere, Garinish and Whiddy to defend the bay.

Prominent along the Cork coastline are several signal towers, now in ruins. Built in the first decade of the 19th century, square or rectangular in shape, they were part of an anti-invasion communications system that stretched along the entire Irish coast. There are good examples at Toe Head, Beara and Mizen Peninsula.

Gate Lodge to Dunboy Castle, Beara

BII

In
pla
Cur
Oys
The
Cou
Ros
alwa
with
In s
and
Gre
for
ies.
Curl
Reds
The
also

Signal Tower at Rock Island, Mizen

Oyste

BUTTERFLIES
and
MOTHS

Over thirty species of butterfly have been observed in West Cork. Some species, like the Clouded Yellow, Painted Lady, Red Admiral and Small Tortoiseshell, migrate from the European continent and can often be seen feeding on ragwort. The Gatekeeper butterfly is confined almost exclusively to the south of Ireland and is widespread in West Cork in coastal areas. The large and colourful Hawkmoths are abundant in summer. Many species migrate from Europe and may be seen in summer in south-easterly winds.

Gatekeeper Butterfly

Six-spotted Burnet Moth

Peacock Butterfly

Clouded Yellow Butterfly

Small Tortoiseshell Butterfly

Painted Lady Butterfly

Red Admiral Butterfly

Emperor Moth

Speckeled Wood Butterfly

Buff-tip Moth

Wall Brown Butterfly

Small Copper Butterfly

Green-veined White Butterfly

Elephant Hawkmoth

Green Hairstreak Butterfly

FLORA
of
SPECIAL INTEREST

The flora of West Cork is one of the most remarkable of any region in Ireland and has several species of special interest among the trees, ferns and wildflowers.

There are a number of rare plant species in West Cork from two different biogeographical groups, American and Lusitanian.

The American group is represented by Blue-eyed Grass, Irish Lady's Tresses Orchid and Irish St. John's Wort. It is believed they have survived from the time when Ireland and America were part of the same landmass.

The Lusitanian species reached West Cork before the last Ice Age from Lusitania (Spain and Portugal). Species include Greater Butterwort, Irish Spurge, Kidney Saxifrage, Kerry Lily, St. Patrick's Cabbage and Strawberry Tree. A number of species that grow in this part of south-west Ireland are not found in Britain.

Blue-eyed Grass

BLUE-EYED GRASS
(Sisyrinchium bermudiana)
This grass-like plant with a tiny blue flower grows in wettish meadows and damp places by roadsides and lakes. The blue flowers appear in June and July. This American wildflower grows mainly in s.w. Ireland.

GREATER BUTTERWORT
(Pinguicula grandiflora)
This summer-flowering insectivorous plant grows in soils poor in nutrients. The plant captures small flies on its sticky leaves and absorbs nourishment from the juices. It grows in peaty ground on Beara, Mizen and a few other places in Ireland. Unknown in Britain and in Europe it grows in the Alps and the south-west.

Fly Agaric Fungus

CAMOMILE (Anthemis nobilis)
The daisy-like Camomile is a low growing perennial which is pleasantly fragrant when the leaves are crushed. The flowers which appear in July and August can be used fresh or dry to make tea. Camomile grows wild in waste places and roadsides and is found in Ireland mainly in West Cork and the south west.

St. Patrick's Cabbage

Betony, grows on Beara but is rare in Ireland.

St. PATRICK'S CABBAGE *(Saxifraga spathularis)*

St. Patrick's Cabbage (also called London Pride), Kidney and Starry Saxifrage, are three species of Saxifrage widespread in West Cork and s.w. Ireland but scarce elsewhere. Flowering between May and July, it grows in damp and rocky places, particularly in the mountains.

Irish Spurge

IRISH SPURGE
(Euphorbia hyberna)

In Ireland the Irish Spurge grows only in the south-west. It is particularly common in West Cork in fields, on banks, along the roadsides and flowers from late April to July.

SPOTTED ROCKROSE
(Tuberaria guttata)

This low-growing wildflower is highly attractive with petals of deep yellow and a blotch of brown. It flowers in May and June but the stems are weak and the flowers fall to the ground on the morning they open. Hence the best time to look for the flower is early morning. It grows mainly in the Mizen area.

Golden Rod

Spotted Rock Rose

Kidney Vetch (normal colouring)

Kidney Vetch (Pink variety, unique to West Cork)

The Kerry Lily grows only in Beara and Kerry.

Three-cornered Leek

Yellow Bartsia

Water Lobelia, grows in lake margins

Greater Butterworth

STRAWBERRY TREE
(Arbutus unedo)

The strawberry-like fruits are edible but tasteless, take one full year to ripen and appear in October along with the new flowers.

This Lusitanian species is one of only two native ever-green-broadleaf-trees that grow in Ireland. It grows mainly in Glengarriff and Killarney Woods and the south west. Not occuring in Britain, in Europe it grows along the Mediterranean.

Strawberry Tree

WILDFLOWERS

Furze

Honeysuckle or Woodbine

Wood Anemone

Rhododendron

West Cork has one of the richest floras of any region of Ireland. From early spring to late autumn it displays a great variety of colourful wildflowers.

The mild climate brings an early spring and so the flowering season begins much sooner for many wild-flower species than elsewhere in Ireland.

Common wildflowers can be seen in a range of habitats such as hedgerows, woodlands, coastal areas and waste ground.

SPRING and SUMMER FLOWERS

In spring the local woodlands come alive with a wide selection of wildflowers including Bluebell, Violet, Wood Anemone and Wood Sorrel. Meanwhile the hedgerows abound with the yellow flowers of the Primrose and Lesser Celandine.

In summer the region is ablaze with brightly coloured wildflower species including Bird's-foot Trefoil, Foxglove and Montbretia.

Montbretia

Sea Pink

COASTAL WILDFLOWERS

Many wildflowers decorate coastal regions in spring and summer. Species to watch out for include Sea Pink, Kidney Vetch, Sea Bindweed, Sea Campion and Sea Holly.

Ragged Robin

Foxglove

Sea Campion

Buttercup

MONTBRETIA (Crocosmia crocosmiflora)

Montbretia has narrow, sword-shaped leaves, grows to 1 metre tall and has bright orange flowers which are a common sight in July and August. A hybrid of two species of *Crocosmia* introduced from South Africa, it was grown for the first time in France in 1880. It was brought to Ireland as a garden plant and spread to hedgebanks and streams throughout West Cork.

FUCHSIA (Fuchsia magellanica)

The Fuchsia is a bushy shrub with very distinctive red-and-purple drooping flowers. From May to October the eye-catching flowers of the Fuchsia adorn the hedgerows throughout West Cork. This shrub, native to South America, was introduced to these islands in the early 19th century and widely planted in western Ireland.

Stonecrop

Fuchsia

White Water Lilly

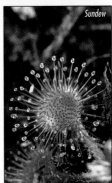

Sundew

WILDLIFE

Hedgehog

Bumble-bee

Few places in Ireland can rival West Cork for variety and rarity of wildlife. West Cork has many habitats including dairy pastures, heathland, hedgerows, mountain, river valley, woodland and a coastline of cliff, dunes, estuary and shingle.
This great variety of habitats and climatic factors leads to a high diversity of wildlife.
The countryside of West Cork contains a superb variety of birds, butterflies and moths, insects, mammals and wild plants. The coastal areas have a rich variety of marine life.

Lesser Horseshoe Bats

KERRY SLUG *(Geomalacus maculosus)*
The Kerry Slug, abundant in parts of West Cork and s.w. Ireland. Elsewhere it is found only in Portugal.

Bank Vole

Ladybird

Common Lizard

MAMMALS

Common species in the West Cork area include Badger, Bank Vole, Bats, Fox, Hare, Hedgehog, Mink, Rabbit, Stoat and the secretive Pine Marten which may be seen occasionally.

Along the coast it is not unusual to see Basking Sharks, Common and Grey Seals, Dolphins and Whales.

Dolphins

Badgers

Pine Marten

WALKING

With its spectacular scenery, quiet country lanes, golden beaches, clean fresh air and solitude, West Cork is ideal walking country. Some favourite places for walking include:
beaches at Ballydonegan, Barleycove, Ownahincha, Long Strand, Red Strand, Warren and many more. Offshore islands of Bere, Cape Clear, Dursey, Sherkin and Whiddy.
Woodland walks at Castlefreke, Glengarriff, Gougane Barra and Lough Hyne.

MARKED WALKING ROUTES

West Cork has two marked, long-distance walking routes, the Beara Way and the Sheep's Head Way. Both are located on peninsulas and take the walker through some of the most glorious wild-countryside of West Cork and Ireland. The Beara Way links up with the Kerry Way at Kenmare.

The BEARA WAY

Beara, a large peninsula in south-west Ireland, is shared between counties Cork and Kerry.

The Beara Way is a long-distance walking route that takes the walker around the Beara Peninsula. The trail does not have an official start or finish. It follows old roads and tracks for some 200km throughout the peninsula and covers some of the most exceptional mountain and coastal scenery in Ireland.

Also it includes sections on the islands of Bere and Dursey. Dursey Island is connected to the mainland by Ireland's only cable car.

Maps of the Beara Way route are available locally or through tourist offices. The O'Sullivan Bere Way meets with the Beara Way in places.

Maps O.S. 1:50,000 Discovery Sheets 84 & 85.

Lough Hyne

Hungry Hill, Beara Way

Gougane Barra Wood

SHEEP'S HEAD WAY

The Sheep's Head Way is some 90km (55mi) long and takes the walker around the Sheep's Head Peninsula. It is a loop walk, beginning officially at Wolf Tone Square in Bantry town. The walk passes historic Bantry House before leading along the northern side of the peninsula, to Sheep's Head, then back along the southern side to Bantry.

This lovely circuit route takes in the panoramic splendour of Bantry Bay and Dunmanus Bay.

Maps O.S. 1:50,000 Discovery Sheets 85 & 88.

A guide to the Sheep's Head Way which includes a map can be purchased locally.

CAPE CLEAR ISLAND

Cape Clear has its own way-marked walk.

It is a short easy walk, confined to the public road-way with numbered posts corresponding to a guide map that indicates the history and culture of this unique place.

Quiet country road in West Cork

Coast of West Cork

Index